SOPHISTICATED STYLE

Who would have dreamed that something as traditional as a crocheted afghan could add elegance to today's clean and modern décor?

Only a designer as creative as Barbara Shaffer could create such beautiful afghans with their theme of contemporary elegance designed to add a touch of colorful excitement to any room.

Whether your color scheme calls for *Really Red*, *Gorgeously Green*, *Beautiful Blue*, *Tempting Taupe* or *Artistic Aran*, these afghans will add that warm designer touch to your home.

LEISURE ARTS, INC.
Little Rock, Arkansas

ARTISTIC ARAN

Finished Size: 53" x 74" (134.5 cm x 188 cm)

■■□□□ **EASY +**

MATERIALS

Medium Weight Yarn ◎④ MEDIUM

[3¹/₂ ounces, 163 yards
(100 grams, 149 meters) per skein]: 19 skeins
Crochet hook, size I (5.5 mm) **or** size
needed for gauge

GAUGE: One Square = 7" (17.75 cm)

STITCH GUIDE

BACK POST DOUBLE CROCHET
(abbreviated BPdc)
YO, insert hook from **back** to **front** around post
of st indicated *(Fig. 3, page 19)*, YO and pull up a
loop (3 loops on hook), (YO and draw through
2 loops on hook) twice.

FRONT POST TREBLE CROCHET
(abbreviated FPtr)
YO twice, insert hook from **front** to **back** around
post of st indicated *(Fig. 3, page 19)*, YO and
pull up a loop (4 loops on hook), (YO and draw
through 2 loops on hook) 3 times.

BEGINNING POPCORN (uses one st or sp)
Ch 3 (**counts as first dc**), 3 dc in st or sp
indicated, drop loop from hook, insert hook
from **front** to **back** in first dc of 4-dc group, pick
up dropped loop and pull through st, ch 1 to
tighten st.

POPCORN (uses one st or sp)
4 Dc in st or sp indicated, drop loop from hook,
insert hook from **front** to **back** in first dc of
4-dc group, pick up dropped loop and pull
through st, ch 1 to tighten st.

SQUARE (Make 70)

Ch 4; join with slip st to form a ring.

Rnd 1 (Right side)**:** Ch 6 (**counts as first dc plus ch 3**),
dc in ring, ch 1, ★ (dc, ch 3, dc) in ring, ch 1; repeat
from ★ 2 times **more**; join with slip st to first dc: 8 dc
and 8 sps.

Note: Loop a short piece of yarn around any stitch to
mark Rnd 1 as **right** side.

Rnd 2: Ch 1, turn; (hdc in next ch-1 sp, 5 hdc in next
ch-3 sp) around; join with slip st to first hdc: 24 hdc.

Rnd 3: Ch 3 (**counts as first dc, now and throughout**),
turn; working in BLO *(Fig. 1, page 19)*, dc in next 2 hdc,
(3 dc, ch 1, 3 dc) in next hdc, ★ dc in next 5 hdc, (3 dc,
ch 1, 3 dc) in next hdc; repeat from ★ 2 times **more**,
dc in last 2 hdc; join with slip st to first dc: 44 dc and
4 corner ch-1 sps.

Rnd 4: Ch 1, do **not** turn; work FPtr around same st as
joining, work BPdc around each of next 5 dc, 3 sc in
next corner ch-1 sp, work BPdc around each of next
5 dc, ★ work FPtr around next dc, work BPdc around
each of next 5 dc, 3 sc in next corner ch-1 sp, work BPdc
around each of next 5 dc; repeat from ★ 2 times **more**;
join with slip st to first FPtr: 56 sts.

Rnd 5: Working in both loops, work Beginning Popcorn
in same st as joining, skip next 2 sts, (dc, ch 3, dc) in
next st, skip next 2 sts, dc in next sc, (2 dc, ch 3, 2 dc)
in next sc, dc in next sc, skip next 2 sts, (dc, ch 3, dc)
in next st, skip next 2 sts, ★ work Popcorn in next st,
skip next 2 sts, (dc, ch 3, dc) in next st, skip next 2 sts,
dc in next sc, (2 dc, ch 3, 2 dc) in next sc, dc in next sc,
skip next 2 sts, (dc, ch 3, dc) in next st, skip next 2 sts;
repeat from ★ 2 times **more**; join with slip st to top of
Beginning Popcorn: 40 dc, 4 Popcorns, and 12 ch-3 sps.

Instructions continued on page 4.

2

Rnd 6: Working in BLO, ch 3, dc in next dc and in next 3 chs, dc in next 4 dc, (2 dc, ch 2, 2 dc) in next corner ch-3 sp, dc in next 4 dc, dc in next 3 chs and in next dc, ★ dc in next Popcorn, dc in next dc and in next 3 chs, dc in next 4 dc, (2 dc, ch 2, 2 dc) in next corner ch-3 sp, dc in next 4 dc, dc in next 3 chs and in next dc; repeat from ★ 2 times **more**; join with slip st to first dc, finish off: 84 dc (21 dc on each side) and 4 corner ch-2 sps.

ASSEMBLY
Join 2 Squares together as follows:

With **right** sides together and working through **both** thicknesses, join yarn with sc in first corner ch-2 sp *(see Joining With Sc, page 19)*; working through **outside** loops on **both** pieces, sc in next 21 dc, sc in next corner ch-2 sp; finish off.

Join remaining Squares, forming 7 vertical strips of 10 Squares each; then join strips together in same manner.

EDGING
Rnd 1: With **right** side facing, join yarn with slip st in any corner ch-2 sp; work Beginning Popcorn in same sp, (ch 2, work Popcorn in same sp) twice, skip next dc, (dc, ch 3, dc) in next dc, [skip next 2 dc, work Popcorn in next dc, skip next 2 dc, (dc, ch 3, dc) in next dc] 3 times, ★ † skip next 2 corner ch-2 sps and next dc on next Square, (dc, ch 3, dc) in next dc, [skip next 2 dc, work Popcorn in next dc, skip next 2 dc, (dc, ch 3, dc) in next dc] 3 times †, repeat from † to † across to next corner ch-2 sp, work Popcorn in corner ch-2 sp, (ch 2, work Popcorn in same sp) twice, skip next dc, (dc, ch 3, dc) in next dc, [skip next 2 dc, work Popcorn in next dc, skip next 2 dc, (dc, ch 3, dc) in next dc] 3 times; repeat from ★ 2 times **more**, then repeat from † to † across; join with slip st to top of Beginning Popcorn: 272 dc, 114 Popcorns, and 144 sps.

Rnd 2: (Slip st, work Beginning Popcorn) in next ch-2 sp, ch 2, work Popcorn in same sp, ch 2, work (Popcorn, ch 2) twice in next ch-2 sp, [(dc, ch 3, dc) in next ch-3 sp, work Popcorn in next Popcorn] 3 times, ★ † (dc, ch 3, dc) in each of next 2 ch-3 sps, work Popcorn in next Popcorn, [(dc, ch 3, dc) in next ch-3 sp, work Popcorn in next Popcorn] twice †, repeat from † to † across to within one ch-3 sp of next corner 3-Popcorn group, (dc, ch 3, dc) in next ch-3 sp, ch 2, work (Popcorn, ch 2) twice in each of next 2 ch-2 sps, [(dc, ch 3, dc) in next ch-3 sp, work Popcorn in next Popcorn] 3 times; repeat from ★ 2 times **more**, then repeat from † to † across to last ch-3 sp, (dc, ch 3, dc) in last ch-3 sp, ch 2; join with slip st to top of Beginning Popcorn: 272 dc, 118 Popcorns, and 156 sps.

Rnd 3: (Slip st, work Beginning Popcorn) in next ch-2 sp, ch 2, work Popcorn in same sp, ch 2, (dc, ch 3, dc) in next ch-2 sp, ch 2, work (Popcorn, ch 2) twice in next ch-2 sp, skip next ch-2 sp, [(dc, ch 3, dc) in next ch-3 sp, work Popcorn in next Popcorn] 3 times, ★ † (dc, ch 3, dc) in each of next 2 ch-3 sps, work Popcorn in next Popcorn, [(dc, ch 3, dc) in next ch-3 sp, work Popcorn in next Popcorn] twice †, repeat from † to † across to within 2 sps of next corner 4-Popcorn group, (dc, ch 3, dc) in next ch-3 sp, ch 2, skip next ch-2 sp, work (Popcorn, ch 2) twice in next ch-2 sp, (dc, ch 3, dc) in next ch-2 sp, ch 2, work (Popcorn, ch 2) twice in next ch-2 sp, skip next ch-2 sp, [(dc, ch 3, dc) in next ch-3 sp, work Popcorn in next Popcorn] 3 times; repeat from ★ 2 times **more**, then repeat from † to † across to last 2 sps, (dc, ch 3, dc) in next ch-3 sp, ch 2, skip last ch-2 sp; join with slip st to top of Beginning Popcorn, finish off.

BEAUTIFUL BLUE

Shown on page 7.

Finished Size: 54" x 70" (137 cm x 178 cm)

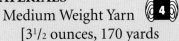 EASY +

MATERIALS
Medium Weight Yarn 〔4〕
[3¹/₂ ounces, 170 yards
(100 grams, 156 meters) per skein]: 21 skeins
Crochet hook, size I (5.5 mm) **or** size
needed for gauge

GAUGE: One Square = 8" (20.25 cm)

STITCH GUIDE

BEGINNING POPCORN (uses one st or sp)
Ch 3 (**counts as first dc**), 3 dc in st or sp
indicated, drop loop from hook, insert hook
from **front** to **back** in first of 4-dc group, pick up
dropped loop and pull through st, ch 1 to tighten
st.

POPCORN (uses one st or sp)
4 Dc in st or sp indicated, drop loop from hook,
insert hook from **front** to **back** in first dc of
4-dc group, pick up dropped loop and pull
through st, ch 1 to tighten st.

BACK POST DOUBLE CROCHET
(*abbreviated BPdc*)
YO, insert hook from **back** to **front** around post
of st indicated (*Fig. 3, page 19*), YO and pull up a
loop (3 loops on hook), (YO and draw through
2 loops on hook) twice.

FRONT POST DOUBLE CROCHET
(*abbreviated FPdc*)
YO, insert hook from **front** to **back** around post
of st indicated (*Fig. 3, page 19*), YO and pull up a
loop (3 loops on hook), (YO and draw through
2 loops on hook) twice.

SQUARE (Make 48)
Ch 4; join with slip st to form a ring.

Rnd 1 (Right side): Work Beginning Popcorn in ring,
(dc, ch 3, dc) in ring, ★ work Popcorn in ring, (dc, ch 3,
dc) in ring; repeat from ★ 2 times **more**; join with
slip st to top of Beginning Popcorn: 8 dc, 4 Popcorns,
and 4 ch-3 sps.

Note: Loop a short piece of yarn around any stitch to
mark Rnd 1 as **right** side.

Rnd 2: Ch 1, turn; 3 hdc in same Popcorn as joining,
skip next dc, (2 hdc, ch 1, 2 hdc) in next ch-3 sp, skip
next dc, ★ 3 hdc in next Popcorn, skip next dc, (2 hdc,
ch 1, 2 hdc) in next ch-3 sp, skip next dc; repeat from ★
2 times **more**; join with slip st to first hdc: 28 hdc and
4 ch-1 sps.

Rnd 3: Ch 3 (**counts as first dc**), turn; dc in BLO of next
2 hdc (*Fig. 1, page 19*), (2 dc, ch 2, 2 dc) in next corner
ch-1 sp, ★ dc in BLO of next 7 hdc, (2 dc, ch 2, 2 dc) in
next corner ch-1 sp; repeat from ★ 2 times **more**, dc in
BLO of last 4 hdc; join with slip st to first dc: 44 dc and
4 corner ch-2 sps.

Rnd 4: Ch 2, do **not** turn; work FPdc around same st as
joining, (work BPdc around next dc, work FPdc around
next dc) twice, 3 sc in next corner ch-2 sp, ★ work FPdc
around next dc, (work BPdc around next dc, work FPdc
around next dc) 5 times, 3 sc in next corner ch-2 sp;
repeat from ★ 2 times **more**, (work FPdc around next
dc, work BPdc around next dc) 3 times; join with slip st
to first FPdc: 56 sts.

Instructions continued on page 6.

Rnd 5: Working in both loops, work Beginning Popcorn in same st as joining, ch 2, skip next st, (work Popcorn in next st, ch 2, skip next st) twice, (dc, ch 2) twice in next corner sc, ★ skip next st, (work Popcorn in next st, ch 2, skip next st) 6 times, (dc, ch 2) twice in next corner sc; repeat from ★ 2 times **more**, skip next st, (work Popcorn in next st, ch 2, skip next st) 3 times; join with slip st to top of Beginning Popcorn: 24 Popcorns, 8 dc, and 32 ch-2 sps.

Rnd 6: Ch 1, **turn**; 2 hdc in each of next 4 ch-2 sps, (2 hdc, ch 2, 2 hdc) in next ch-2 sp, ★ 2 hdc in each of next 7 ch-2 sps, (2 hdc, ch 2, 2 hdc) in next ch-2 sp; repeat from ★ 2 times **more**, 2 hdc in each of last 3 ch-2 sps; join with slip st to first hdc: 72 hdc and 4 ch-2 sps.

Rnd 7: Ch 1, do **not** turn; hdc in same st as joining and in each hdc around working 5 hdc in each corner ch-2 sp; join with slip st to first hdc, finish off: 92 hdc.

ASSEMBLY

Join 2 Squares together as follows:

With **right** sides together, working through **both** thicknesses and in **outside** loops on **both** pieces, join yarn with sc in center hdc of corner 5-hdc group (see *Joining With Sc, page 19*); sc in next 23 hdc; finish off.

Join remaining Squares, forming 6 vertical strips of 8 Squares each; then join strips together in same manner.

EDGING

Rnd 1: With **right** side facing and working in BLO, join yarn with dc in center hdc of any corner 5-hdc group (see *Joining With Dc, page 19*); ch 1, 2 dc in same st, ★ dc in next 22 hdc, [dc in same hdc as joining on same Square and in same st as joining on next Square, dc in next 22 hdc] across to center hdc of next corner 5-hdc group, (2 dc, ch 1, 2 dc) in center hdc; repeat from ★ 2 times **more**, dc in next 22 hdc, [dc in same hdc as joining on same Square and in same st as joining on next Square, dc in next 22 hdc] across, dc in same st as first dc; join with slip st to first dc: 680 dc and 4 ch-1 sps.

Rnd 2: Slip st in next ch-1 sp, ch 5 (**counts as first dc plus ch 2**), 2 dc in same sp, ★ (work FPdc around next dc, work BPdc around next dc) across to next corner ch-1 sp, (2 dc, ch 2, 2 dc) in corner sp; repeat from ★ 2 times **more**, (work FPdc around next dc, work BPdc around next dc) across, dc in same sp as first dc; join with slip st to first dc: 696 sts and 4 ch-2 sps.

Rnd 3: Slip st in next ch-1 sp, ch 4 (**counts as first dc plus ch 1**), (dc, ch 3, dc) in same sp, ★ † skip next 2 sts, [(dc, ch 3, dc) in next st, skip next 3 sts] across to next corner ch-2 sp †, (dc, ch 3, dc, ch 1, dc, ch 3, dc) in corner sp; repeat from ★ 2 times **more**, then repeat from † to † once, dc in same sp as first dc, ch 3; join with slip st to first dc: 360 dc and 184 sps.

Rnd 4: Slip st in next corner ch-1 sp, ch 3, ★ (dc, ch 3, dc) in each ch-3 sp across to next corner ch-1 sp, dc in corner sp; repeat from ★ 2 times **more**, (dc, ch 3, dc) in each ch-3 sp across; join with slip st to first dc: 180 ch-3 sps.

Rnd 5: Turn; slip st in next dc, ch 1, 5 hdc in next ch-3 sp and in each ch-3 sp around; join with slip st to first hdc, finish off.

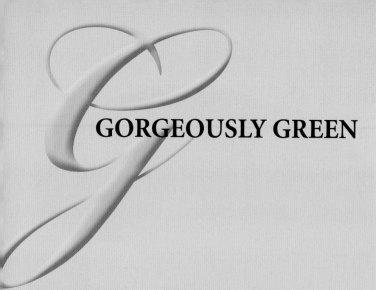

GORGEOUSLY GREEN

Finished Size: 52" x 69" (132 cm x 175.5 cm)

◼◼◻◻ EASY

MATERIALS

Medium Weight Yarn 〔4〕 MEDIUM
[5 ounces, 256 yards
(140 grams, 234 meters) per skein]: 14 skeins
Crochet hook, size I (5.5 mm) **or** size
needed for gauge

GAUGE: In pattern, one repeat (19 sts) = 5" (12.75 cm)

STITCH GUIDE

BACK POST DOUBLE CROCHET
(abbreviated BPdc)
YO, insert hook from **back** to **front** around post of
st indicated *(Fig. 3, page 19)*, YO and pull up a loop
(3 loops on hook), (YO and draw through 2 loops
on hook) twice.

FRONT POST DOUBLE CROCHET
(abbreviated FPdc)
YO, insert hook from **front** to **back** around post of
st indicated *(Fig. 3, page 19)*, YO and pull up a loop
(3 loops on hook), (YO and draw through 2 loops
on hook) twice.

BODY

Ch 179, place a marker in third ch from hook to mark
edging placement.

Row 1: Dc in fourth ch from hook (**3 skipped chs count
as first dc**) and in next 3 chs, skip next 2 chs, (2 dc,
ch 1, 2 dc) in next ch, [skip next 4 chs, (2 dc, ch 1, 2 dc)
in next ch] twice, ★ skip next 2 chs, dc in next 4 chs,
skip next 2 chs, (2 dc, ch 1, 2 dc) in next ch, [skip next
4 chs, (2 dc, ch 1, 2 dc) in next ch] twice; repeat from
★ across to last 7 chs, skip next 2 chs, dc in last 5 chs:
150 dc and 27 ch-1 sps.

Row 2 (Right side)**:** Ch 3 (**counts as first dc, now and
throughout**), turn; dc in BLO of next 4 dc (*Fig. 1,
page 19*), skip next dc, work 2 FPdc around next dc, sc
in next ch-1 sp, work 2 FPdc around next dc, skip next
dc, work BPdc around each of next 2 dc, sc in next
ch-1 sp, work BPdc around each of next 2 dc, skip next
dc, work 2 FPdc around next dc, sc in next ch-1 sp, work
2 FPdc around next dc, ★ skip next dc, dc in BLO of
next 4 dc, skip next dc, work 2 FPdc around next dc, sc
in next ch-1 sp, work 2 FPdc around next dc, skip next
dc, work BPdc around each of next 2 dc, sc in next
ch-1 sp, work BPdc around each of next 2 dc, skip next
dc, work 2 FPdc around next dc, sc in next ch-1 sp, work
2 FPdc around next dc; repeat from ★ across to last
6 dc, skip next dc, dc in BLO of last 5 dc: 177 sts.

Row 3: Ch 3, turn; working in both loops, dc in next
4 dc, ch 2, skip next 2 sts, dc in next sc, (ch 4, skip next
4 sts, dc in next sc) twice, ★ ch 2, skip next 2 sts, dc in
next 4 dc, ch 2, skip next 2 sts, dc in next sc, (ch 4, skip
next 4 sts, dc in next sc) twice; repeat from ★ across to
last 7 sts, ch 2, skip next 2 sts, dc in last 5 dc: 69 dc and
36 sps.

8

Instructions continued on page 10.

Row 4: Ch 1, turn; sc in BLO of first 5 dc, skip next ch-2 sp, (5 sc in **both** loops of next dc, skip next sp) 3 times, ★ sc in BLO of next 4 dc, skip next ch-2 sp, (5 sc in **both** loops of next dc, skip next sp) 3 times; repeat from ★ across to last 5 dc, sc in BLO of last 5 dc: 177 sc.

Row 5: Ch 3, turn; working in both loops, dc in next 4 sc, skip next 2 sc, (2 dc, ch 1, 2 dc) in next sc, [skip next 4 sc, (2 dc, ch 1, 2 dc) in next sc] twice, ★ skip next 2 sc, dc in next 4 sc, skip next 2 sc, (2 dc, ch 1, 2 dc) in next sc, [skip next 4 sc, (2 dc, ch 1, 2 dc) in next sc] twice; repeat from ★ across to last 7 sc, skip next 2 sc, dc in last 5 sc: 150 dc and 27 ch-1 sps.

Rows 6-122: Repeat Rows 2-5, 29 times; then repeat Row 2 once **more**; do **not** finish off: 177 sts.

EDGING

Rnd 1: Ch 4 (**counts as first dc plus ch 1, now and throughout**), do **not** turn; 2 dc in both loops of last dc on Row 122 of Body; working in end of rows, skip first row, (dc, ch 3, dc) in next row, [skip next 2 rows, (dc, ch 3, dc) in next row] twice, † skip next row, (dc, ch 3, dc) in next row, [skip next 2 rows, (dc, ch 3, dc) in next row] twice †; repeat from † to † across to last 2 rows, skip last 2 rows; working in free loops of beginning ch (*Fig. 2, page 19*), (2 dc, ch 1, 2 dc) in marked ch, skip next 2 sts, (dc, ch 3, dc) in next st, ♥ [skip next 4 sts, (dc, ch 3, dc) in next st] 3 times, skip next 3 sts, (dc, ch 3, dc) in next st ♥; repeat from ♥ to ♥ across to last 2 sts, skip next st, (2 dc, ch 1, 2 dc) in last st; working in end of rows, skip first 2 rows, (dc, ch 3, dc) in next row, [skip next 2 rows, (dc, ch 3, dc) in next row] twice, ★ skip next row, (dc, ch 3, dc) in next row, [skip next 2 rows, (dc, ch 3, dc) in next row] twice; repeat from ★ across to last row, skip last row; working in sts across Row 122 of Body, (2 dc, ch 1, 2 dc) in first dc, skip next 2 sts, (dc, ch 3, dc) in next st, repeat from ♥ to ♥ across to last st, skip last st, dc in same st as first dc; join with slip st to first dc: 344 dc and 168 sps.

Rnd 2: (Slip st, ch 4, 3 dc) in next corner ch-1 sp, ★ ch 4, (dc in next ch-3 sp, ch 4) across to next corner ch-1 sp, (3 dc, ch 1, 3 dc) in corner sp; repeat from ★ 2 times **more**, ch 4, (dc in next ch-3 sp, ch 4) across, 2 dc in same sp as first dc; join with slip st to first dc: 188 dc and 172 sps.

Rnd 3: (Slip st, ch 4, dc) in next corner ch-1 sp, ★ † dc in BLO of next 3 dc, dc in next 4 chs, (skip next dc, dc in next 4 chs) across to within 3 dc of next corner ch-1 sp, dc in BLO of next 3 dc †, (dc, ch 1, dc) in corner sp; repeat from ★ 2 times **more**, then repeat from † to † once; join with slip st to first dc: 704 dc and 4 ch-1 sps.

Rnd 4: (Slip st, ch 4, dc) in next corner ch-1 sp, ★ (work FPdc around next dc, work BPdc around next dc) across to next corner ch-1 sp, (dc, ch 1, dc) in corner sp; repeat from ★ 2 times **more**, (work FPdc around next dc, work BPdc around next dc) across; join with slip st to first dc: 712 sts and 4 ch-1 sps.

Rnd 5: (Slip st, ch 4, dc) in next corner ch-1 sp, ch 1, ★ (skip next st, dc in BLO of next st, ch 1) across to next corner ch-1 sp, (dc, ch 1) twice in corner sp; repeat from ★ 2 times **more**, (skip next st, dc in BLO of next st, ch 1) across; join with slip st to first dc: 364 dc and 364 ch-1 sps.

Rnd 6: (Slip st, ch 4, 2 dc) in next corner ch-1 sp, ★ dc in BLO of next dc, (dc in next ch, dc in BLO of next dc) across to next corner ch-1 sp, (2 dc, ch 1, 2 dc) in corner sp; repeat from ★ 2 times **more**, dc in BLO of next dc, (dc in next ch, dc in BLO of next dc) across; join with slip st to first dc: 740 dc and 4 ch-1 sps.

Rnd 7: (Slip st, ch 4, dc) in next corner ch-1 sp, work FPdc around next dc, ★ (work BPdc around next dc, work FPdc around next dc) across to next corner ch-1 sp, (dc, ch 1, dc) in corner sp, work FPdc around next dc; repeat from ★ 2 times **more**, (work BPdc around next dc, work FPdc around next dc) across; join with slip st to first dc: 748 dc and 4 ch-1 sps.

Rnd 8: (Slip st, ch 1, 3 sc) in next ch-1 sp, ★ sc in BLO of each st across to next corner ch-1 sp, 3 sc in corner sp; repeat from ★ 2 times **more**, sc in BLO of each st across; join with slip st to first sc, finish off.

TEMPTING TAUPE

Shown on page 13.

Finished Size: 56" x 71½" (142 cm x 181.5 cm)

⬛⬛⬜⬜ **EASY**

MATERIALS
Medium Weight Yarn **4** MEDIUM
  [3½ ounces, 170 yards
  (100 grams, 156 meters) per skein]: 20 skeins
Crochet hook, size I (5.5 mm) **or size**
  needed for gauge

GAUGE: In pattern, 17 sts and 8 rows = 5" (12.75 cm)
  Each Panel = 7½" (19 cm) wide

STITCH GUIDE
BACK POST DOUBLE CROCHET
(abbreviated BPdc)
YO, insert hook from **back** to **front** around post
of st indicated *(Fig. 3, page 19)*, YO and pull up a
loop (3 loops on hook), (YO and draw through
2 loops on hook) twice.
FRONT POST DOUBLE CROCHET
(abbreviated FPdc)
YO, insert hook from **front** to **back** around post
of st indicated *(Fig. 3, page 19)*, YO and pull up a
loop (3 loops on hook), (YO and draw through
2 loops on hook) twice.

PANEL (Make 7)
Ch 19.

Row 1 (Right side)**:** (Dc, ch 3, dc) in sixth ch from hook
(**5 skipped chs count as first dc and 2 skipped chs**),
★ skip next 4 chs, (dc, ch 3, dc) in next ch; repeat from
★ once **more**, skip next 2 chs, dc in last ch: 8 dc and
3 ch-3 sps.

Note: Loop a short piece of yarn around any stitch to
mark Row 1 as **right** side and bottom edge.

Row 2: Ch 3 (**counts as first dc, now and throughout**),
turn; 5 dc in each of next 3 ch-3 sps, skip next dc, dc in
last dc: 17 dc.

Row 3: Ch 3, turn; dc in BLO of next dc and each dc
across *(Fig. 1, page 19)*.

Row 4: Ch 3, turn; work BPdc around next dc, (work
FPdc around next dc, work BPdc around next dc) across
to last dc, dc in last dc.

Row 5: Ch 3, turn; working in both loops, skip next
2 sts, (dc, ch 3, dc) in next st, ★ skip next 4 sts, (dc,
ch 3, dc) in next st; repeat from ★ once **more**, skip next
2 sts, dc in last dc: 8 dc and 3 ch-3 sps.

Rows 6-105: Repeat Rows 2-5, 25 times; do **not**
finish off.

Instructions continued on page 12.

BORDER

Rnd 1: Ch 3, do **not** turn; 4 dc in last dc made on Row 105 (corner); work 2 dc in end of each row across; working in free loops of beginning ch *(Fig. 2, page 19)*, 5 dc in first ch (corner), dc in next 15 chs, 5 dc in next ch (corner); work 2 dc in end of each row across; working in sts on Row 105, 5 dc in first dc (corner), dc in each dc and in each ch across; join with slip st to first dc: 470 dc.

Rnd 2: Ch 1, work FPdc around same st as joining, work BPdc around next dc, (work FPdc around next dc, work BPdc around next dc) around; join with slip st to first FPdc.

Rnd 3: Ch 1, turn; hdc in same st as joining and in next 17 sts, 3 hdc in next st (corner), hdc in next 214 sts, 3 hdc in next st (corner), hdc in next 19 sts, 3 hdc in next st (corner), hdc in next 214 sts, 3 hdc in next st (corner), hdc in last st; join with slip st to first hdc: 478 hdc.

Rnd 4: Ch 1, turn; working in BLO, sc in same st as joining and in next 2 hdc, 3 sc in next corner hdc, ★ sc in next hdc and in each hdc across to center hdc of next corner 3-hdc group, 3 sc in corner hdc; repeat from ★ 2 times **more**, sc in next hdc and in each hdc across; join with slip st to **both** loops of first sc, finish off.

ASSEMBLY

Join long edge of 2 Panels together as follows:

With **right** sides together, bottom edges to your right, and working through **both** thicknesses and in **outside** loops on **both** pieces, join yarn with sc in center sc of corner *(see Joining With Sc, page 19)*; sc in next sc and in each sc across through center sc of next corner; finish off.

Join remaining Panels in same manner.

EDGING

Rnd 1: With **right** side of short edge facing, join yarn with dc in BLO of center sc of first corner 3-sc group *(see Joining With Dc, page 19)*; dc in same st as joining and in BLO of next 23 dc, † [dc in BLO of same st as joining on same Panel and in end of joining sc, dc in BLO of same st as joining on next Panel and in next 23 sc] across to center sc of next corner 3-sc group, 3 dc in BLO of corner sc, dc in BLO of next sc and each sc across to center sc of next corner 3-sc group †, 3 dc in BLO of corner sc, dc in BLO of next 23 dc, repeat from † to † once, dc in BLO of same st as joining; join with slip st to **both** loops of first dc: 806 dc.

Rnd 2: Ch 1, turn; working in both loops, 2 hdc in same st as joining, ★ hdc in next dc and in each dc across to center dc of next corner 3-dc group, 3 hdc in corner dc; repeat from ★ 2 times **more**, hdc in next dc and in each dc across, hdc in same st as joining; join with slip st to first hdc: 814 hdc.

Rnd 3: Ch 1, turn; (sc, ch 2, 2 dc) in same st as joining, skip next 3 hdc, ★ (sc, ch 2, 2 dc) in next hdc, skip next 2 hdc; repeat from ★ around; join with slip st to first sc, finish off.

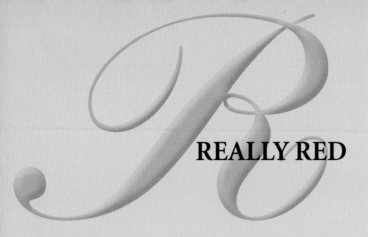

REALLY RED

Finished Size: 51¹/₂" x 72" (131 cm x 183 cm)

 EASY

MATERIALS
Medium Weight Yarn 🧶 **4** MEDIUM
   [6 ounces, 315 yards
   (170 grams, 288 meters) per skein]: 13 skeins
Crochet hook, size I (5.5 mm) **or** size
   needed for gauge

GAUGE: In pattern, 15 hdc = 4" (10 cm);
              Rows 3-18 = 7" (17.75 cm)

STITCH GUIDE

POPCORN (uses one st)
4 Dc in st indicated, drop loop from hook, insert
hook from **front** to **back** in first dc of 4-dc group,
pick up dropped loop and pull through st,
ch 1 to tighten st.

BACK POST DOUBLE CROCHET
   (abbreviated BPdc)
YO, insert hook from **back** to **front** around post of
st indicated *(Fig. 3, page 19)*, YO and pull up a loop
(3 loops on hook), (YO and draw through 2 loops
on hook) twice.

FRONT POST DOUBLE CROCHET
   (abbreviated FPdc)
YO, insert hook from **front** to **back** around post of
st indicated *(Fig. 3, page 19)*, YO and pull up a loop
(3 loops on hook), (YO and draw through 2 loops
on hook) twice.

FRONT POST TREBLE CROCHET
   (abbreviated FPtr)
YO twice, insert hook from **front** to **back** around
post of st indicated *(Fig. 3, page 19)*, YO and pull up
a loop (4 loops on hook), (YO and draw through
2 loops on hook) 3 times. Skip st behind FPtr.

PICOT
Ch 3, sc in third ch from hook.

BODY
Ch 165, place a marker in third ch from hook to mark
edging placement.

Row 1 (Right side)**:** Dc in fourth ch from hook
(**3 skipped chs count as first dc**), skip next 2 chs, work
(Popcorn, ch 2, Popcorn) in next ch, ★ skip next 2 chs,
dc in next 6 chs, ch 2, skip next 2 chs, sc in next ch,
ch 2, skip next 2 chs, dc in next 6 chs, skip next 2 chs,
work (Popcorn, ch 2, Popcorn) in next ch; repeat from
★ across to last 4 chs, skip next 2 chs, dc in last 2 chs:
88 dc, 16 Popcorns, 7 sc, and 22 ch-2 sps.

Row 2: Ch 3 (**counts as first dc, now and throughout**),
turn; work BPdc around next st, skip next Popcorn,
5 hdc in next ch-2 sp, ★ skip next Popcorn, work FPdc
around each of next 2 sts, work BPdc around each of
next 2 sts, work FPdc around each of next 2 sts, skip
next ch-2 sp, (dc, ch 3, dc) in next sc, skip next ch-2 sp,
work FPdc around each of next 2 sts, work BPdc around
each of next 2 sts, work FPdc around each of next 2 sts,
skip next Popcorn, 5 hdc in next ch-2 sp; repeat from
★ across to last 3 sts, skip next Popcorn, work BPdc
around next dc, dc in last dc: 56 FPdc, 30 BPdc, 40 hdc,
16 dc, and 7 ch-3 sps.

Row 3: Ch 1, turn; sc in BLO of first dc *(Fig. 1, page 19)*,
work FPdc around next st, sc in BLO of next 7 sts, work
FPdc around each of next 2 sts, sc in BLO of next 2 sts,
skip next dc, 5 sc in next ch-3 sp, skip next dc, sc in
BLO of next 2 sts, work FPdc around each of next 2 sts,
★ sc in BLO of next 9 sts, work FPdc around each of
next 2 sts, sc in BLO of next 2 sts, skip next dc, 5 sc in
next ch-3 sp, skip next dc, sc in BLO of next 2 sts, work
FPdc around each of next 2 sts; repeat from ★ across to
last 9 sts, sc in BLO of next 7 sts, work FPdc around next
st, sc in BLO of last dc: 133 sc and 30 FPdc.

Instructions continued on page 16.

14

Row 4: Ch 1, turn; hdc in both loops of first st and each st across: 163 hdc.

Row 5: Ch 1, turn; sc in BLO of first hdc, work FPtr around next FPdc one row **below** next hdc, sc in BLO of next 7 hdc, work FPtr around each of next 2 FPdc one row **below** next 2 hdc, ★ sc in BLO of next 9 hdc, work FPtr around each of next 2 FPdc one row **below** next 2 hdc; repeat from ★ across to last 9 sts, sc in BLO of next 7 hdc, work FPtr around next FPdc one row **below** next hdc, sc in BLO of last hdc: 133 sc and 30 FPtr.

Row 6: Ch 3, turn; dc in both loops of next st and each st across: 163 dc.

Row 7: Ch 3, turn; work FPdc around next dc, (work BPdc around next dc, work FPdc around next dc) across to last dc, dc in last dc: 81 FPdc, 80 BPdc, and 2 dc.

Row 8: Ch 1, turn; hdc in both loops of first st and each st across: 163 hdc.

Row 9: Ch 3, turn; working in BLO, dc in next hdc, ch 2, skip next 2 hdc, sc in next hdc, ch 2, ★ skip next 2 hdc, dc in next 6 hdc, skip next 2 hdc, work (Popcorn, ch 2, Popcorn) in next hdc, skip next 2 hdc, dc in next 6 hdc, ch 2, skip next 2 hdc, sc in next hdc, ch 2; repeat from ★ across to last 4 hdc, skip next 2 hdc, dc in last 2 hdc: 88 dc, 8 sc, 14 Popcorns, and 23 ch-2 sps.

Row 10: Ch 3, turn; work BPdc around next dc, skip next ch-2 sp, (dc, ch 3, dc) in both loops of next sc, skip next ch-2 sp, ★ work FPdc around each of next 2 dc, work BPdc around each of next 2 dc, work FPdc around each of next 2 dc, skip next Popcorn, 5 hdc in next ch-2 sp, skip next Popcorn, work FPdc around each of next 2 dc, work BPdc around each of next 2 dc, work FPdc around each of next 2 dc, skip next ch-2 sp, (dc, ch 3, dc) in both loops of next sc, skip next ch-2 sp; repeat from ★ across to 2 dc, work BPdc around next dc, dc in both loops of last dc: 56 FPdc, 30 BPdc, 35 hdc, 18 dc, and 8 ch-3 sps.

Row 11: Ch 1, turn; sc in BLO of first dc, work FPdc around next st, skip next dc, 5 sc in next ch-3 sp, skip next dc, ★ sc in BLO of next 2 sts, work FPdc around each of next 2 sts, sc in BLO of next 9 sts, work FPdc around each of next 2 sts, sc in BLO of next 2 sts, skip next dc, 5 sc in next ch-3 sp, skip next dc; repeat from ★ across to last 2 sts, work FPdc around next st, sc in BLO of last dc: 133 sc and 30 FPdc.

Rows 12-16: Repeat Rows 4-8: 163 hdc.

Row 17: Ch 3, turn; working in BLO, dc in next hdc, skip next 2 hdc, work (Popcorn, ch 2, Popcorn) in next hdc, ★ skip next 2 hdc, dc in next 6 hdc, ch 2, skip next 2 hdc, sc in next hdc, ch 2, skip next 2 hdc, dc in next 6 hdc, skip next 2 hdc, work (Popcorn, ch 2, Popcorn) in next hdc; repeat from ★ across to last 4 hdc, skip next 2 hdc, dc in last 2 hdc: 88 dc, 16 Popcorns, 7 sc, and 22 ch-2 sps.

Row 18: Ch 3, turn; work BPdc around next st, skip next Popcorn, 5 hdc in next ch-2 sp, ★ skip next Popcorn, work FPdc around each of next 2 sts, work BPdc around each of next 2 sts, work FPdc around each of next 2 sts, skip next ch-2 sp, (dc, ch 3, dc) in both loops of next sc, skip next ch-2 sp, work FPdc around each of next 2 sts, work BPdc around each of next 2 sts, work FPdc around each of next 2 sts, skip next Popcorn, 5 hdc in next ch-2 sp; repeat from ★ across to last 3 sts, skip next Popcorn, work BPdc around next dc, dc in both loops of last dc: 56 FPdc, 30 BPdc, 40 hdc, 16 dc, and 7 ch-3 sps.

Rows 19-147: Repeat Rows 3-18, 8 times; then repeat Row 3 once **more** [piece should measures approximately 64" (162.5 cm) from beginning ch]; do **not** finish off.

EDGING

Rnd 1: Ch 4 (**counts as first dc plus ch 1**), do **not** turn; 3 dc in both loops of last sc on Row 147 of Body; working in end of rows, skip first row, ★ 2 dc in next row, dc in next 2 rows, 2 dc in each of next 2 rows, dc in next 3 rows, 2 dc in each of next 2 rows, dc in next row, 2 dc in each of next 2 rows, dc in next 3 rows; repeat from ★ across to last 2 rows, 2 dc in each of last 2 rows; working in free loops (*Fig. 2, page 19*) and in unworked chs of beginning ch, (3 dc, ch 1, 3 dc) in first ch, dc in each ch across to marked ch, (3 dc, ch 1, 3 dc) in marked ch; working in end of rows, 2 dc in each of first 2 rows, † dc in next 3 rows, 2 dc in each of next 2 rows, dc in next row, 2 dc in each of next 2 rows, dc in next 3 rows, 2 dc in each of next 2 rows, dc in next 2 rows, 2 dc in next row †, repeat from † to † across to last row, skip last row; working in both loops of sts across Row 147 of Body, (3 dc, ch 1, 3 dc) in first sc, dc in each st across, 2 dc in same st as first dc; join with slip st to first dc: 768 dc and 4 ch-1 sps.

Rnd 2: (Slip st, ch 1, 2 sc) in next ch-1 sp, ★ work FPdc around next dc, (work BPdc around next dc, work FPdc around next dc) across to next corner ch-1 sp, 3 sc in corner sp; repeat from ★ 2 times **more**, work FPdc around next dc, (work BPdc around next dc, work FPdc around next dc) across, sc in same sp as first sc; join with slip st to first sc: 780 sts.

Rnd 3: Ch 1, **turn**; 2 hdc in same st as joining, ★ hdc in each st across to center sc of next corner 3-sc group, 3 hdc in center sc; repeat from ★ 2 times **more**, hdc in each st across, hdc in same st as first hdc; join with slip st to FLO of first hdc: 788 hdc.

Rnd 4: Ch 3, turn; working in BLO, dc in same st as joining, ★ dc in next hdc and in each hdc across to center hdc of next corner 3-hdc group, 3 dc in center hdc; repeat from ★ 2 times **more**, dc in next hdc and in each hdc across, dc in same st as first dc; join with slip st to first dc: 796 dc.

Rnd 5: Ch 1, do **not** turn; 2 sc in same st as joining, ★ work BPdc around next dc, (work FPdc around next dc, work BPdc around next dc) across to center dc of next corner 3-dc group, 3 sc in center dc; repeat from ★ 2 times **more**, work BPdc around next dc, (work FPdc around next dc, work BPdc around next dc) across, sc in same st as first sc; join with slip st to first sc: 804 sts.

Rnd 6: Ch 1, **turn**; 2 hdc in same st as joining, ★ hdc in next st and in each st across to center sc of next corner 3-sc group, 3 hdc in center sc; repeat from ★ 2 times **more**, hdc in next st and in each st across, hdc in same st as first hdc; join with slip st to first hdc: 812 hdc.

Rnd 7: Ch 6 (**counts as first dc plus ch 3**), turn; dc in same st as joining, † skip next 2 hdc, [(dc, ch 3, dc) in next hdc, skip next 2 hdc] across to center hdc of next corner 3-hdc group, dc in center hdc, (ch 3, dc in same st) twice, skip next 3 hdc †, [(dc, ch 3, dc) in next hdc, skip next 2 hdc] across to center hdc of next corner 3-hdc group, dc in center hdc, (ch 3, dc in same st) twice, repeat from † to † once, [(dc, ch 3, dc) in next hdc, skip next 2 hdc] across, dc in same st as joining, ch 3; join with slip st to first dc.

Rnd 8: Ch 1, do **not** turn; (sc, work Picot) twice in same st as joining, ★ (sc in next ch-3 sp, work Picot) across to center dc of next corner, (sc, work Picot) twice in center dc; repeat from ★ 2 times **more**, (sc in next ch-3 sp, work Picot) across; join with slip st to first sc, finish off.

GENERAL INSTRUCTIONS

ABBREVIATIONS

BLO	Back Loop(s) Only
BPdc	Back Post double crochet(s)
ch(s)	chain(s)
cm	centimeters
dc	double crochet(s)
FLO	Front Loop(s) Only
FPdc	Front Post double crochet(s)
FPtr	Front Post treble crochet(s)
hdc	half double crochet(s)
mm	millimeters
Rnd(s)	Round(s)
sc	single crochet(s)
sp(s)	space(s)
st(s)	stitch(es)
YO	yarn over

★ — work instructions following ★ as many **more** times as indicated in addition to the first time.

† to † or ♥ to ♥ — work all instructions from first † to second † or from first ♥ to second ♥ **as many** times as specified.

( ) or [ ] — work enclosed instructions **as many** times as specified by the number immediately following **or** work all enclosed instructions in the stitch or space indicated **or** contains explanatory remarks.

colon (:) — the number(s) given after a colon at the end of a row or round denote(s) the number of stitches you should have on that row or round.

CROCHET TERMINOLOGY

UNITED STATES		INTERNATIONAL
slip stitch (slip st)	=	single crochet (sc)
single crochet (sc)	=	double crochet (dc)
half double crochet (hdc)	=	half treble crochet (htr)
double crochet (dc)	=	treble crochet(tr)
treble crochet (tr)	=	double treble crochet (dtr)
double treble crochet (dtr)	=	triple treble crochet (ttr)
triple treble crochet (tr tr)	=	quadruple treble crochet (qtr)
skip	=	miss

Yarn Weight Symbol & Names	LACE 0	SUPER FINE 1	FINE 2	LIGHT 3	MEDIUM 4	BULKY 5	SUPER BULKY 6
Type of Yarns in Category	Fingering, 10-count crochet thread	Sock, Fingering Baby	Sport, Baby	DK, Light Worsted	Worsted, Afghan, Aran	Chunky, Craft, Rug	Bulky, Roving
Crochet Gauge* Ranges in Single Crochet to 4" (10 cm)	32-42 double crochets**	21-32 sts	16-20 sts	12-17 sts	11-14 sts	8-11 sts	5-9 sts
Advised Hook Size Range	Steel*** 6,7,8 Regular hook B-1	B-1 to E-4	E-4 to 7	7 to I-9	I-9 to K-10.5	K-10.5 to M-13	M-13 and larger

*GUIDELINES ONLY: The chart above reflects the most commonly used gauges and hook sizes for specific yarn categories.

** Lace weight yarns are usually crocheted on larger-size hooks to create lacy openwork patterns. Accordingly, a gauge range is difficult to determine. Always follow the gauge stated in your pattern.

*** Steel crochet hooks are sized differently from regular hooks–the higher the number the smaller the hook, which is the reverse of regular hook sizing.

CROCHET HOOKS												
U.S.	B-1	C-2	D-3	E-4	F-5	G-6	H-8	I-9	J-10	K-10 ½	N	P	Q
Metric - mm	2.25	2.75	3.25	3.5	3.75	4	5	5.5	6	6.5	9	10	15

■□□□ BEGINNER	Projects for first-time crocheters using basic stitches. Minimal shaping.
■■□□ EASY	Projects using yarn with basic stitches, repetitive stitch patterns, simple color changes, and simple shaping and finishing.
■■■□ INTERMEDIATE	Projects using a variety of techniques, such as basic lace patterns or color patterns, mid-level shaping and finishing.
■■■■ EXPERIENCED	Projects with intricate stitch patterns, techniques and dimension, such as non-repeating patterns, multi-color techniques, fine threads, small hooks, detailed shaping and refined finishing.

GAUGE

Exact gauge is essential for proper size. Hook size given in instructions is merely a guide and should never be used without first making a sample swatch approximately 4" (10 cm) square in the stitch, yarn, and hook specified. Then measure the swatch, counting your stitches and rows or rounds carefully. If your swatch is larger or smaller than specified, **make another, changing hook size to get the correct gauge.** Keep trying until you find the size hook that will give you the specified gauge.

HINTS

As in all crocheted pieces, good finishing techniques make a big difference in the quality of the piece. Make a habit of taking care of loose ends as you work. Thread a yarn needle with the yarn end. With **wrong** side facing, weave the needle through several stitches, then reverse the direction and weave it back through several stitches. When ends are secure, clip them off close to work.

JOINING WITH SC

When instructed to join with sc, begin with a slip knot on the hook. Insert the hook in the stitch or space indicated, YO and pull up a loop, YO and draw through both loops on hook.

JOINING WITH DC

When instructed to join with dc, begin with a slip knot on the hook. YO, holding loop on hook, insert the hook in the stitch or space indicated, YO and pull up a loop (3 loops on hook), (YO and draw through both loops on hook) twice.

BACK OR FRONT LOOP ONLY

Work only in loop(s) indicated by arrow (*Fig. 1*).

Fig. 1

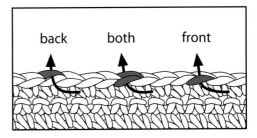

FREE LOOPS OF A CHAIN

When instructed to work in free loops of a chain, work in loop indicated by arrow (*Fig. 2*).

Fig. 2

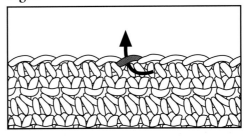

POST STITCH

Work around the post of stitch indicated, inserting the hook in the direction of arrow (*Fig. 3*).

Fig. 3

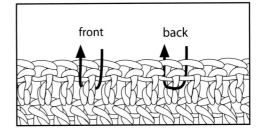

YARN INFORMATION

Each Afghan in this leaflet was made using Medium Weight Yarn. Any brand of Medium Weight Yarn may be used. It is best to refer to the yardage/meters when determining how many balls or skeins to purchase. Remember, to arrive at the finished size, it is the GAUGE/TENSION that is most important, not the brand of yarn.

For your convenience, listed below are the specific yarns used to create our photo models.

ARTISTIC ARAN
Bernat® Satin
#04007 Silk

BEAUTIFUL BLUE
Lion Brand® Yarn Vanna's Choice®
#109 Colonial Blue

GORGEOUSLY GREEN
Red Heart® Soft Yarn®
#9522 Leaf

TEMPTING TAUPE
Lion Brand® Yarn Vanna's Choice®
#125 Taupe

REALLY RED
Caron® Simply Soft®
#9730 Autumn Red

Production Team: Writer/Technical Editor - Linda Daley; Editorial Writer - Susan McManus Johnson; Senior Graphic Artist - Lora Puls; and Graphic Artists - Jacob Casleton and Janie Wright.

For digital downloads of Leisure Arts' best-selling designs, visit http://leisureartslibrary.com